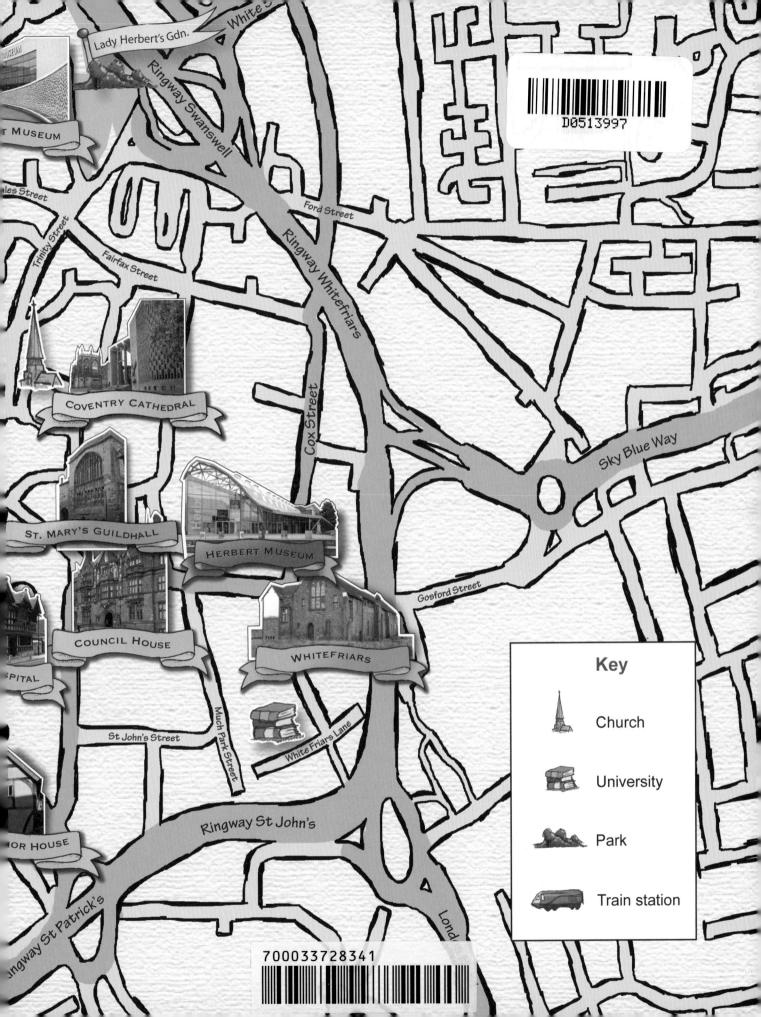

Lady Herbert's Gdn.

White S...

Ringway Swanswell

...les Street

Trinity Street

Fairfax Street

Ford Street

Ringway Whitefriars

Cox Street

Sky Blue Way

COVENTRY CATHEDRAL

ST. MARY'S GUILDHALL

HERBERT MUSEUM

Gosford Street

...OR MUSEUM

...t MUSEUM

COUNCIL HOUSE

WHITEFRIARS

...SPITAL

St John's Street

Much Park Street

White Friars Lane

...OR HOUSE

Ringway St John's

Ringway St Patrick's

Lond...

D0513997

Key

Church

University

Park

Train station

children's HISTORY of COVENTRY

Written by
Ann Evans

HOMETOWN WORLD

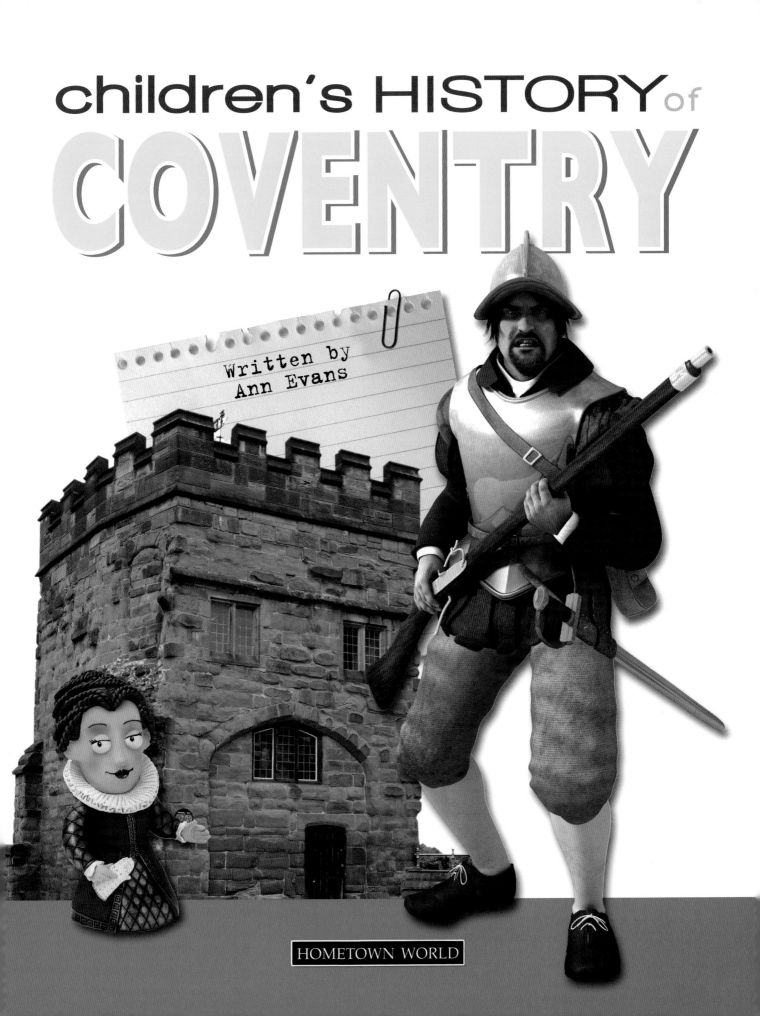

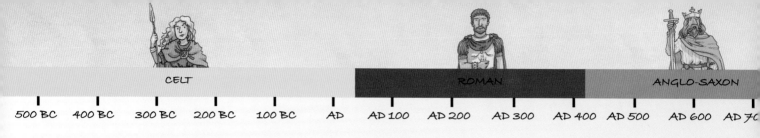

CELT   ROMAN   ANGLO-SAXON

500 BC   400 BC   300 BC   200 BC   100 BC   AD   AD 100   AD 200   AD 300   AD 400   AD 500   AD 600   AD 70

How well do you know your town?

Have you ever wondered what it would have been like living in Coventry when Lady Godiva was there? What about being a silk-weaver for the rich factory owners in Georgian times? This book tells the story of your town, with all the important and exciting things that have happened there.

Want to hear the other good bits? You will love this book! Some rather brainy folk have worked on it to make sure it's fun and informative. So what are you waiting for? Peel back the pages and be amazed at what happened in your town.

THE FACTS

Timeline shows which period (dates and people) each spread is talking about

Clear informative text

'Spot this!' game with hints on something to find in your town

THE EVIDENCE

Go back in time to read what it was like for children growing up in Coventry.

Each period in the book ends with a summary explaining how we know about the past.

Intriguing old photos

Hometown facts to amaze you!

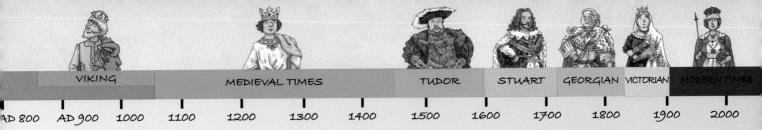

Contents

CELT
500 BC

ROMAN
AD 43-410

ANGLO-
SAXON
AD 450-
1066

VIKING
AD 865-
1066

MEDIEVAL
TIMES
1066-
1485

A Bloody Battle

Standing guard on the Lunt Fort's tall wooden ramparts, overlooking huge forests of oak trees, Gallius spies something moving. The troops are returning. They are bringing horses and ponies with them. He shouts in triumph, guessing they are horses taken as booty from Boudicca's Iceni tribe after their bloodied defeat. Excitedly, Gallius calls for the fort's gateway to be opened wide to allow them entry.

The Romans are hard taskmasters – they train us for marching and for battle. But they feed us well!

The gyrus, a large circular arena just inside the main fort, was probably used to train horses for the Roman army.

Cofa's Tree

Long before Roman times, Coventry was known as Cofa's Tree, or Couaentree. It was a clearing in the huge Forest of Arden close to the River Sherbourne. Local people grazed their cattle and sheep there and the marshy Babba Lacu provided plenty of fish. Part of this lake still survives at Swanswell Pool near the city centre.

But in AD 43 Claudius, Emperor of Rome, invaded Britain with his 40,000-strong army. Battles raged as Roman troops spread through the country. The Roman Governor of Britain, Suetonius Paulinus, ordered the Lunt Fort to be built at Baginton on the edge of Coventry. It was used as a training ground for the cavalry.

A bloody battle took place around AD 60–61 close to present-day Coventry. The Romans fought with the local Celts led by Boudicca, queen of the Iceni tribe. Rather than be captured, Boudicca took her own life by poison. Her many horses and ponies were probably taken to the Lunt Fort to be trained for the Roman army.

Defending the Fort

The Lunt Roman Fort was built at a crossing point of the River Sowe some distance from the junction of two Roman roads, the Fosse Way and Watling Street. The Lunt Roman Fort was built from turf and timber with tall ramparts and two lines of V-shaped ditches all around. The Roman word for ditch was *fossae*. It could be up to 6 metres wide and 2.5 metres deep. These ditches were very narrow at the bottom so they were nicknamed 'ankle-breakers'.

At the bottom of the ditches were wooden stakes and metal spikes. There would also be brambles and nettles on the slopes. If invaders got past all that and reached the ramparts of the fort, the walls had narrow slots in them — perfect for a Roman sword to slide through.

The Lunt Fort was rebuilt three or four times over the centuries that the Romans occupied Britain.

The word 'Lunt' refers to trees and wooded slopes.

SPOT THIS!

The Lunt Roman Fort at Baginton, just outside Coventry, has been partially rebuilt to show how it would have been around AD 64.

Life with the Romans

After the Roman conquest, most Britons worked on the land just as before and were still ruled by local chiefs. Some British tribes lived peacefully alongside the Romans — as long as they paid the Roman taxes.

But slowly life began to change for everyone. The chiefs began to dress in the Roman fashion and speak Latin. The Romans introduced their own gods and goddesses and the Britons came to worship these alongside their own gods and goddesses of nature and the seasons.

The Romans made improvements. They built good roads and bridges, and introduced a new building material — concrete. Personal hygiene improved too, as the Romans used hot baths, lavatories and sewers to take away the waste.

When the Roman army left in AD 410 to defend Rome against barbarian invasions, some soldiers stayed here, marrying local girls and settling down.

You're all less smelly now that we've brought better lavatories and sewers.

I love your ideas about food. Who would have thought of a three-course meal?

...AD 60-61 Boudicca defeated...AD 410 Romans leave Britain...

5

CELT
500 BC

ROMAN
AD 43-410

ANGLO-
SAXON
AD 450-
1066

VIKING
AD 865-
1066

MEDIEV
TIMES
1066-
1485

Marcus is 10 years old. His father is Keeper of the Armaments at the Lunt Fort. Because he is high ranking, Marcus lives in the *praetorium* and has lessons with a tutor every day. Here's an imaginary diary entry.

> When I'm 20, I'll be old enough to fight the local Iceni and Silurians if they still rebel.

Dies Lunae (Monday)

This morning I spent at my studies with my tutor, Phaedrus. First I did writing practice on my wax tablet, some arithmetic and then I had my lesson in public speaking. I did well and Phaedrus didn't beat me.

This afternoon, I will take riding lessons at the *gyrus*. The gyrus is a 34-metre circular arena where our cavalry train – horses and men. It is important to ride well and learn to control these native horses as I hope to lead the cavalry when I'm older.

I have my riding lesson while the soldiers rest on bunks or relax and play board games in the *papilio*. Each century of 80 men has its own barracks. They sleep six men to a room. They snack on oysters in there too, so the whole place smells horrid!

After riding I will have some free time. I'm allowed to help out at the stable block feeding the horses hay from the *horrea*. Our corn is kept here too. The *horrea* are built on stilts so the air can circulate. The walls are sealed from insects and rodents with *amurca*, which is left over from processing olives.

Speaking of olives, I'm hungry, it must be lunchtime!

PLAN OF THE LUNT ROMAN FORT

- ■ fabricae (workshop)
- ■ defences
- ■ gyrus (arena) and stables
- ■ gateway
- ■ horreum (granary)
- ■ principia (headquarters)
- ■ praetorium (officers' living quarters)
- ■ papilio (soldiers' barracks)

How do we know?

In the 1960s, archaeologists uncovered the foundations of a Roman fort at Baginton, near Coventry, so we know about the layout of the fort. Post holes give us an idea of how the gates, defences and buildings were constructed. The circular gyrus together with pieces of Roman armour and horse equipment support the idea that the Roman cavalry trained horses there. You can see re-enactments of life in the Roman fort at the Lunt Roman Fort.

Many of the artefacts found during the excavations at the Lunt Roman Fort are now in the Herbert Art Gallery and Museum, Coventry.

A Roman historian called Tacitus wrote about the battle against Boudicca. He reported that no fewer than 80,000 Britons were put to the sword, while the Romans lost about 400 soldiers. He also records that Boudicca ended her life with a dose of poison.

The Lunt Fort was an important centre in Roman Britain.

The Roman camp was like a small town, with engineers, carpenters, masons, wagon-makers, blacksmiths, painters and others skilled people. Women and children lived there too.

The 'scorpione' is a crossbow that fires 20-cm iron bolts.

Lady Godiva

It is time. Countess Godigfu mounts her horse and passes her cloak to her handmaid. The maid lowers her eyes. With only her long flowing hair to cover her modesty, Godigfu – or Godiva – rides slowly through Coventry's empty streets. The air is cold against her naked skin. The only sound is the clatter of hooves against cobbles. No one peeps, for which she is thankful.

The name Godiva means 'God's gift'.

The Anglo-Saxon Chronicle describes Leofric as 'wise for God and the World'.

Invaders and Settlers

Around 1035, Godigfu, or Godiva as we know her, was married to Leofric, a high-ranking Anglo-Saxon. The Anglo-Saxons took over Britain after the Romans left, dividing the country into small kingdoms.

In AD 893, another army of invaders arrived. The Vikings from Scandinavia conquered the north-east of England settling in the area which became known as the Danelaw. Coventry was just outside the Danelaw in the Kingdom of Merica.

In 1016 the Viking King Canute appointed Leofric Earl of Mercia. He was one of King Canute's close and trusted friends. Leofric became one of the three most powerful men in the country.

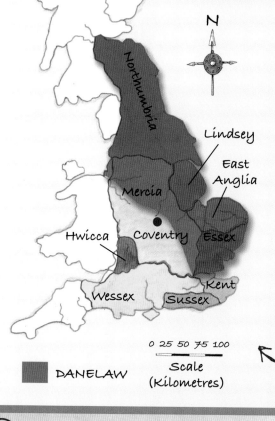

This map shows the old Anglo-Saxon kingdoms and the Danelaw.

N

Northumbria

Lindsey

East Anglia

Mercia

Hwicca

Coventry

Essex

Wessex

Sussex

Kent

DANELAW

0 25 50 75 100
Scale (Kilometres)

King Canute's Tax

According to legend, Godiva worried that Coventry people had to pay a 'heregeld' land tax, which paid for King Canute's bodyguard. Godiva had no authority to reduce this tax herself but begged Leofric to do so. Leofric told Godiva that if she rode naked through the streets of Coventry he would lift the tax from Coventry citizens. He probably never expected her to do so, but Godiva did just that – and marked her place in history forever.

In a later version of the story, a tailor peeped through a hole in his window shutters as Lady Godiva passed by. He was struck blind and became known as Peeping Tom. This likeness of Peeping Tom is in Hertford Street.

St Mary's Priory

Godiva and Leofric founded a Benedictine priory for 24 monks in 1043. There had already been a nunnery on the same spot, built in AD 670 by Saint Osberga. But the nunnery was destroyed by the Vikings in around 1016. Godiva and Leofric built their priory on the ruins close to where the Cathedral stands today, just to the side of Trinity Church in Priory Row. By 1102 it was known as the Priory and Cathedral of St Mary's. It survived for just over 400 years.

Leofric kept his word and lifted the hated heregeld land tax. But he still had a tax on horses.

SPOT THIS!

There are statues of Lady Godiva all over Coventry. Can you spot this one? Clue: Look in St Mary's Guildhall.

The excavated ruins of St Mary's Priory reveal vaulted ceilings, windows and a fireplace. Some stonework appears to be over 1,000 years old!

CELT
500 BC

ROMAN
AD 43-410

ANGLO-
SAXON
AD 450-
1066

VIKING
AD 865-
1066

MEDIEVA
TIMES
1066-
1485

Leofa is 10 years old. She lives in Coventry with her mother, father, grandparents and brother Berhtulf. Here is an imaginary account, though she would not have been able to read or write.

My name, Leofa, means 'deer' and my brother's name, Berhtulf, means 'bright wolf'.

Mona, 1045

Berhtulf and I went with Mother and Father to the market today. Berhtulf helped Father drive the sheep. Mother and I took wool and honey to sell. We have a bee hive in our village. We keep a big flock of sheep. Berhtulf and I look after them with our father and our dogs. Our wool is very important. We keep some and the women spin it and weave the yarn into cloth on looms. I'm quite good at that too.

I love going to market. It grows bigger each time I go. Traders from all over the country bring their goods to the gates of Godiva's Priory. St Mary's church is so beautiful. It is made of stone, and inside it glitters with gold and silver and gemstones. When we came home there was smoke rising with a delicious smell coming from the hut. Grandmother had cooked a broth of vegetables and poached fish that Grandfather had caught in the River Sherbourne. We were so tired and hungry it made our mouths water.

Come closer, while I whisper something to you. There was a rumour going round at the market – Countess Godiva took off all her clothes and rode naked through the streets! They say she did it to stop the dreadful heregeld tax. Everyone had to stay indoors and not peep as she rode past. It's a good job she has very long hair, that's all I can say!

The Viking house was made from timber and thatch. It had one room with a dirt floor spread with rushes. In the centre a cooking pot hung above an open fire. The smoke escaped through a hole in the roof.

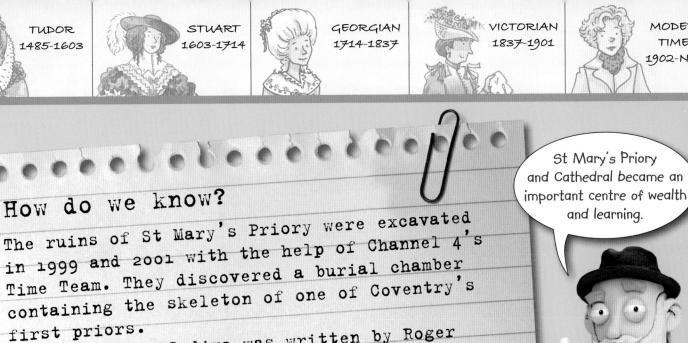

How do we know?

The ruins of St Mary's Priory were excavated in 1999 and 2001 with the help of Channel 4's Time Team. They discovered a burial chamber containing the skeleton of one of Coventry's first priors.

The story of Godiva was written by Roger of Wendover 120 years after the event in his Flores Historiarum (Flowers of History). However, he was well known for stretching the truth. There is no firm evidence that she ever rode through the streets naked!

About the same time that Lady Godiva was in Coventry, the population would have been at least 400. We know this from the Domesday Book which was compiled by monks in 1086. It was a survey of the whole country, listing anything of value.

You can still find some Anglo-Saxon place names in Coventry. Cross Cheaping is an Anglo-Saxon name for Market Cross.

St Mary's Priory and Cathedral became an important centre of wealth and learning.

The English days of the week are named after Saxon and Viking gods.

An office has been built over St Mary's Priory but you can still explore the undercroft and cloister garden at the Visitors' Centre in Priory Row.

English	Saxon
Monday	Mona
Tuesday	Tiu
Wednesday	Woden
Thursday	Thor
Friday	Freya
Saturday	Sæternesdæg
Sunday	Sunne

CELT
500 BC

ROMAN
AD 43-410

ANGLO-
SAXON
AD 450-
1066

VIKING
AD 865-
1066

MEDIEVA
TIMES
1066-148

Coventry Fair

"Come feel my fine cloth! It's the best blue you can buy in Coventry," the cloth merchant calls to the passers-by. The fair is open and Coventry is filled with merchants, weavers, spinners, farmers and, of course, monks from St Mary's Benedictine Priory. The streets are piled high with sacks of wool for sale. There is a rumour that the prior has just sold 300 sacks. That should keep the woollen mills busy!

Alas! The priory has lost its power and the guilds have grown wealthy.

Some people believe that Caesar's Tower, in the corner on the right, is all that is left of Coventry Castle.

Market Town

Coventry once had a castle in Broadgate. It was built around 1090 by the Earl of Chester. But it didn't last long – King Stephen tore it down in 1136 during the Barons' War.

The small town of Coventry grew up in two halves. The people living around St Mary's Priory worked for the prior. The Earl's tenants, living around Cheylesmore Manor, were freer to trade. In 1154, King Henry II gave Coventry a royal charter granting the right to hold an annual fair. By this time, Coventry was the fifth largest town in England. It was selling wool and cloth all over Europe.

In 1345, King Edward III granted the town a charter to hold its own town council and three years later, Coventry elected its first Lord Mayor, John Ward. The following year, a dreadful plague struck the citizens of Coventry - the Black Death. It was a disease carried by rat fleas that had spread around Britain. It killed a large number of people including many monks and Prior William Irreys himself. The town came under the control of the Corporation and Queen Isabella who owned Cheylesmore Manor. A 'murage' tax was raised to build a town wall. Building began in 1355 and Coventry town wall was one of the finest in the country. It was 4 metres high, 2.5 metres thick, and had 20 towers and 12 gates. But it took almost 180 years to build!

TUDOR
1485-1603

STUART
1603-1714

GEORGIAN
1714-1837

VICTORIAN
1837-1901

MODERN
TIMES
1902-
NOW

Duel of Gosford Green

Thousands flocked to Gosford Green on St Lamath's Day, 17th September, 1398. Richard II had proclaimed a 'trial by combat' between Henry Bolingbroke, Duke of Hereford, and Thomas Mowbray, Duke of Norfolk. Both men had accused each other of treason but as neither the king nor Parliament could decide who was guilty they were committed to trial by duel.

As the two dukes prepared to charge, King Richard suddenly stopped the duel. After two hours, the king decided to exile the dukes instead, Bolingbroke for 10 years and Mowbray for life. Their lands were confiscated.

A year later, Bolingbroke returned, took the king prisoner and forced him to give up the throne. The king was killed soon after and Bolingbroke became Henry IV. As for Mowbray, he died in exile.

Thousands of people who flocked to Gosford Green to see the duel went home disappointed.

St Mary's Guildhall

As trade grew, so the traders organized themselves into guilds which became the Trinity Guild. St Mary's Guildhall, opened in 1342, was a meeting place for the Merchant Guild of St Mary. It also became the headquarters for the mayor and Corporation right up until the 1900s when Coventry Council House was built.

King Henry VI held court in the Guildhall during the Wars of the Roses.

Cheylesmore Manor – once a royal manor house of King Edward II, Queen Isabella and her grandson, the Black Prince – is now a registry office.

SPOT THIS!

The original Coventry Cross was put up in the marketplace in 1423. It cost £50. Today, a new Coventry Cross stands between Cuckoo Lane and Holy Trinity just 100 metres from where the original stood.

Tristana is 12 years old. Her father is an important wool merchant living in Gosford Street. He belongs to the powerful Trinity Guild and is a member of the town council.

We use sloe berries to make our blue dye - it doesn't wash out. But don't tell!

Holy Cross Day, 14th September, 1456:
Today, King Henry VI and his Queen, Margaret of Anjou, and many noblemen including the Duke of York, paraded into Coventry through Spon Gate. It was such a pageant! Parliament is being held in Coventry again. It's so exciting!

15th September, 1456:
Father was angry today. The murage tax was due which pays for the upkeep of our town wall. But someone (it wasn't us) has thrown human waste (poo) into the ditch at the other side of the wall, and now we've been fined – it's not fair!

16th September, 1456:
It was market day today. I helped my father sell our cloth. A merchant from Oxford tried to trick me into telling him our recipe for blue dye. But it's top secret. We have a saying: "as true as Coventry Blue".

17th September, 1456:
This evening I went to meet Father from the Guild meeting. He let me peep inside St Mary's Guildhall - it's so grand and beautiful!
As we walked home, we could see the three spires of St Michael, Holy Trinity and Christ Church. I love Coventry!

You can find out how John Croke the weaver lived in 1540 at the Weaver's House in Spon End.

The old Council Chamber inside St Mary's Guildhall.

The huge Coventry Tapestry still hangs in St Mary's Guildhall on the wall where it has hung for 500 years.

How do we know?

We know about Coventry Castle from the documents that record the life of the castle but not much is known about what it looked like. The ruins of the castle probably lie beneath St Mary's Guildhall.

St Mary's Guildhall had many famous visitors including Mary Queen of Scots and William Shakespeare played there several times.

The Coventry Tapestry, which hangs in St Mary's Guildhall, shows King Henry VI, his wife Margaret of Anjou and other important people. It was woven between 1495 to 1500.

There are still traces of the wool trade in Coventry's street names, such as Mill Lane and Draper's Hall.

Trade grew so rapidly that by 1465 Coventry had its own mint to make halfpennies.

You can still explore the town wall at Swansgate.

15

St Mary's Destroyed

On 15th January, 1539, Bishop Roland Lee and Thomas Camswell, prior of St Mary's Cathedral, bravely face King Henry VIII's men. They try to stop them destroying the Cathedral and Priory.

"Our orders come from the King himself," growls one of the king's men. "The country answers to His Majesty now, not the Pope."

"This church was founded by Godiva and Leofric," pleads the Bishop. "It has stood for 500 years..."

"I have my orders!" says the king's officer. "Stand aside!"

I'm head of the church in England now, so I'm entitled to keep its power and wealth!

SPOT THIS!

You can read the names of the Coventry Martyrs on a memorial close to the spot where they died in Cheylesmore. The last three burned at the stake in 1555.

Royal Visitors

King Henry VIII visited Coventry with his queen, Catherine of Aragon, in 1510. Twenty years later, Henry wanted to divorce her. This caused an argument with the pope in Rome who was head of the church. Henry decided to make himself head of the Church of England, closed down the abbeys and monasteries, and siezed their land and treasure. In 1539, Whitefriars and Greyfriars monasteries, and St Mary's Church and its abbey were all seized by the king. Later the same year, the smaller St Anne's Charterhouse on the London Road was also closed.

Coventry Martyrs

Henry VIII wasn't the only one to question the authority of the church in Rome. In Coventry, followers of John Wycliffe, called the Lollards, had their own ideas of how the church should be run and thought it should pay tax too! Between 1510 and 1555, eleven Lollards were burnt at the stake for their beliefs. They are still remembered as the Coventry Martyrs today.

TUDOR
1485-1603

STUART
1603-1714

GEORGIAN
1714-1837

VICTORIAN
1837-1901

MODERN
TIMES
1902-NOW

John Hales

In 1545, St Mary's Church was bought by John Hales. He was a Member of Parliament and it was his job to collect church revenues for King Henry VIII. Hales also bought Whitefriars monastery and made it his home. After King Henry died, his daughter Queen Elizabeth I visited Coventry and spoke to its citizens from the Oriel window of Whitefriars in 1565.

Hales started a free grammar school in Hales Street in 1572. The building still stands in Hales Street, but the school later moved to Warwick Row where it became known as King Henry VIII School.

The Oriel window of Whitefriars monastery close to the junction of Gulson Road and London Road is now part of the museum.

Wealthy Merchants

John Hales was only one of Coventry's great benefactors. A wealthy draper and former mayor of Coventry, Thomas Bond, founded Bond's Hospital and Bablake Boys' School in 1506. And in 1509, William Ford founded Ford's Hospital, or almshouse, for elderly people.

Bond's Hospital and Bablake School buildings are still lived in today, almost 500 years later.

In 1569, Elizabeth I had her cousin Mary Queen of Scots imprisoned in St Mary's, most likely in Caesar's Tower.

Civil War

When civil war broke out in 1642, Coventry supported the Parliamentarians. The city walls proved too strong for King Charles I's Royalist forces. Although they blew a hole in New Gate, the local people filled the gap with rubble and the Royalists gave up. Royalist troops captured in the north in 1646 were 'sent to Coventry' to be kept prisoner in St John's Church. Perhaps in revenge, 16 years later King Charles II sent 500 men to destroy the city wall leaving only the gates and towers standing. It took just three weeks to knock down a wall that took 179 years to build.

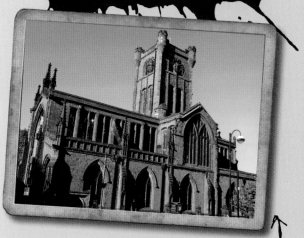

A plaque on St John the Baptist Church records the Royalists imprisoned in the Civil War.

CELT 500 BC	ROMAN AD 43-410	ANGLO-SAXON AD 450-1066	VIKING AD 865-1066	MEDIEVAL TIMES 1066-148

Benjamin Clark is almost 11 years old. Like his father, he makes leather clothes, saddles and purses. He's the youngest of five brothers and sisters. He can read and write, as he is a pupil at the Free Grammar School in Hales Street. He lives in Spon Street. Here is his imaginary diary entry.

> I'm glad the Civil War is over. Grandad says there were no pageants or plays back then. Even the maypoles were taken down!

31st May, 1678

There's a new family moved in next door. I saw the girl yesterday. She nodded to me so I nodded back. Mum says they're French Huguenots who have run away from their own country so that they can worship in their own way. They are very skilled weavers. In their house they have their own single-shuttle hand loom and make beautiful silk ribbons. It is the fashion now for well bred gentlemen and ladies to decorate their clothing with ribbons.

I'm closing the journal now because the Great Show Fair is on in Coventry and the Godiva Procession is about to start. Four 'waits' will play their instruments and lead the procession in their fine cloaks wearing the city's badge. Oh, by the way, our 'Godiva' leading the procession is Mayor Swinnerton's son and a medal is struck in commemoration. He will be wearing all his clothes... I hope!

A terrible plague swept through the country during the early 1600s. It reached Coventry in May 1603 killing 494 people.

Cook Street Gate is one of only two of the original town gates that survive. The other one is Swanswell Gate.

> As the power of the church grew weaker, the power of the guilds and merchants grew stronger.

A bomb fell on Ford's Hospital during World War Two and caused a lot of damage. The building has since been restored. →

How do we know?

We still have documents which record events from this time. A copy of a letter from Queen Elizabeth I to the people of Coventry is kept in St Mary's Guildhall.

John Foxe's Book of Martyrs includes illustrations of religious martyrs being burned at the stake.

The parish register at Mucklestone for 1604 records: 'Note that this yere was a Universall plage.' It then lists a number of places including 'The cyty of Coventry'.

The Coventry Leet Book, which was the mayor's register, records the duties of the 'waits' musicians in the Godiva Procession. The Godiva Festival is still held every July.

Elizabeth R   By the Quene

Trust and well beloved we grete you well. Forasmuche as wee have for dyvers good consideration given orders to our right trusty and right welbeloved Cousyns the Earles of Shrewsbury and Huntington to bring the Scottyshe Queene to that our towne of Coventrie and here to see her safely kept and garded untyll our pleasure shall be otherwise to determine. We let you will our pleasure and commandment is that for the better assystance of our sayd Cousyns and either of them in this charge committed unto them, you shall from tyme to tyme followe such order and direction, as shall for that purpose bee by them or either of them prescribed unto you in such wyse as they or either of them shall think fit for the weale and furtherance of our service.

Yeven under our Signet at our Castle of Wyndsyr the xxvith of November xiith yere of our Reigne

Steam Looms

The noise and steam from the engine frightens me. It works the new ribbon weaving looms allowing us to weave many ribbons rather than just one at a time. I dream of attending school but my family needs my wage. I am lucky, some children work down coal mines or are chimney sweeps. At least I can see the sky through the big windows of our weaver's cottage and work until the light fades.

By the end of the 1800s, Coventry had 248 cycle companies and employed around 40,000 people!

The Cash brothers built these homes for their workers alongside the canal. Today they are luxury apartments.

Industrial Revolution

Coventry was the centre of ribbon weaving in England and it was the city's main industry. Around 1770, new coal-powered steam looms were introduced. They could weave many ribbons at one time. These steam engines were the start of the Industrial Revolution.

Two Quaker brothers, John and Joseph Cash, built well-lit top floors to the weavers' cottages at Kingfield and put in Jacquard looms powered by a central beam engine. J & J Cash Ltd was a huge success, producing ribbons, badges and labels.

Clocks

In 1727 a watchmaker named George Porter became mayor of Coventry. Growth of this skilled industry grew rapidly. Watchmakers, such as Bonniksen, worked from home in their workshops at the upstairs back of the house, known as 'top shops'. Rotherhams in Spon Street were known for their highly skilled craftsmen. By the late 1700s, Coventry was one of the three main centres in England for watch and clock manufacture.

...1769 COVENTRY CANAL OPENS...1838 COVENTRY STATION OPENS...

A Growing City

Coal was needed to power the new steam revolution. Many coal pits were sunk around the city. Coventry Canal was built to carry coal and other goods to where they were needed. In 1769 the Coventry Canal Basin near the town centre was opened. This had expanded to Hawksbury Junction on the outskirts by 1788. Then, in 1838, the railway arrived, stopping at Coventry Station on the way from London to Birmingham.

The railway and the canal brought more trade to Coventry. As industry grew so did the population. The medieval town gates were demolished to allow room for traffic. In 1820 a gasworks opened in Coventry and soon there were gas lights on the streets. The rest of the city stayed much the same with its medieval buildings and houses.

SPOT THIS!

Can you spot this mosaic along the Canal walk? The elephant and castle and the cat-a-mountain are part of the city's coat of arms.

Cycles and Motorcars

Based on the French-designed bone-shaker, James Starley built the first penny-farthing in about 1871. This new method of transport was built at the Coventry Machinists Company, where Starley also made sewing machines.

The first British motor car was produced by the Daimler Motor Company. The man leading the new industry was Harry Lawson, an inventor, who took over an old cotton mill in Radford in 1896 and renamed it Motor Mills. Lawson said he chose Coventry because the skills used in the watch, cycle and sewing machine trades were needed to make cars.

> Coventry was a centre of industry making cloth, clocks, cycles and cars.

By Her Majesty's Royal Letters Patent

THE "ARIEL" BICYCLE.

Fitted with Lever Tension Wheels, India Rubber Tyres, Improved Radder, Registered Cliptail Sliding Spring, &c.

SMITH, STARLEY, & CO.,
PATENTEES & MANUFACTURERS,
ST. AGNES WORKS, COVENTRY.

You can see James Starley's penny-farthing at Coventry Transport Museum.

The Workhouse

Some people grew very rich during the boom years. But as cheap imports of cloth and watches arrived from abroad, many people lost their jobs. Whitefriars monastery became the Coventry Workhouse in 1801. At first it was known as the 'House of Industry' providing work, clothing and food for the poor. In 1834 the Poor Law Act was passed, and conditions at the Workhouse became worse to discourage poor people from seeking help.

Alice used to be a silk-weaver But the mechanized looms are so efficient, the mills need fewer workers. So now Alice is in the workhouse where poor people are sent when they cannot earn enough money for rent. Here's an entry from her imaginary diary:

Have you heard, George Eliot probably based her book Middlemarch on her life in Coventry.

Tuesday 15th June, 1858

Today I could forget my woes. I went down to the station to join the huge crowds waiting to see Queen Victoria and Prince Albert arrive at Coventry Station. The station was decorated with banners and evergreens and the platform spread with a crimson cloth. As the Queen and the Prince Consort stepped from the train a royal salute was fired, the church bells rang and the crowds cheered. Then the Queen was surrounded by a guard of honour and I couldn't see her any more – she's smaller than I'd thought! Anyway, after all the excitement and waiting I was feeling a bit flat, when I spied something abandoned on the ground. It was a Thomas Stevens woven-silk bookmark commemorating the Queen's visit! I shall treasure this forever!

THERE ARE NO PRIZES

For the following Couplet :

"To have accurate returns of time and speed
A BONNIKSEN Speedmeter is what you need."

But the possession of this ultra-reliable type of Speedometer will ensure a winning chance of a Prize in Competitions and Trials. It will be found to give invaluable assistance and is also a proved companion on tour.

Prices :
MOTORCYCLE TYPE :—
Trip. £5   Non-Trip. £4 - 10
(Rear Drive for American Machines 10s. extra.)
CAR or CYCLECAR
TYPE :   Trip, £6 - 10
         Non-Trip. £6
TIME-SPEEDMETER :—
Motorcycle Type,   Car Type, £8
£6 - 10
Send for Illustrated Booklet.

Rotherham & Sons, Ltd., Coventry.

Telephone—752 and 753.   Telegrams—" Rotherhams, Coventry."

Bonniksen was a watchmaker who lived in Norfolk Street. He used his skills to improve the motorcycle speedometer.

Thomas Stevens invented a process for weaving elaborate pictures in silk known as Stevengraphs. They became very popular.

TUDOR 1485-1603

 STUART 1603-1714

 GEORGIAN 1714-1837

 VICTORIAN 1837-1901

 MODERN TIMES 1902-NOW

Harry Lawson's Motor Manufacturing Company around 1898. Lawson also owned Daimler and organized the first London to Brighton car run in 1896.

In 1885, John Kemp Starley, nephew of James Starley, manufactured a bicycle with a chain-driven rear wheel and equal-sized wheels. The bicycle became known as the Rover.

WATCH THIS SPACE
IN FUTURE FOR
STARLEY & SUTTON'S ANNOUNCEMENTS
Lord Bury rides the "Rover."

THE BEST WINTER CYCLE EXTANT. NO SKIDDING OR SIDE-SLIPPING, AND NO FEAR OF FALLS.

FASTER THAN A BICYCLE, AND SAFER THAN A TRICYCLE. UNDOUBTEDLY THE MACHINE OF THE FUTURE.

The ROVER Bicycle
(Patented and Registered.)

Price Lists, Testimonials, etc.—including one from the Right Honourable Viscount Bury, President of the National Cyclists' Union—post free.

STARLEY & SUTTON, METEOR WORKS, WEST ORCHARD, COVENTRY, ENGLAND.

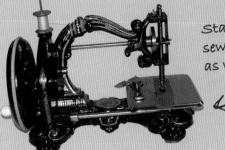

Starley made sewing machines as well as cycles.

How do we know?

In 1741, Coventry had its first newspaper - Jopson's Coventry Mercury. Then came the Coventry Gazette and Birmingham Chronical in 1757 and Piercy's Coventry Gazette in 1777-1778 followed by the Coventry Herald in 1808. Newspapers carried advertisements for the new technology of the day. Starley and Singer bicycles are displayed at Coventry Transport Museum along with old posters advertising them. Visit London Road Cemetery where you can find a memorial to James Starley and other famous Coventry people.

London Illustrated News **19ᵗʰ June, 1858**

Arrival at Coventry
The Royal train, consisting of seven carriages, left the station at Euston Square at three o'clock and, stopping only at Bletchley for a few minutes, arrived at Coventry at half past five, the hour indicated in the time-table. There, an immense concourse of the citizens had stood for hours, exposed to the glare of a burning sun, to catch a sight of the Queen. The station was profusely decorated with banners and evergreens and the platform spread with crimson cloth. As the cortége entered the station, a Royal salute was fired from a battery expressly sent from Weedon for the occasion; the city bells were rung and the crowd raised an enthusiastic cheer.

The Blitz

Thousands of incendiary bombs have fallen on Coventry. The city is ablaze. I am the Cathedral provost, Richard T Howard, and I'm standing here helpless, watching our beloved Cathedral burn. It feels as if I am watching the crucifixion of Jesus on his cross.
This is how Richard T Howard described the events of 14th November, 1940 in his diary.

Fire from incendiary bombs spread rapidly through the city's medieval streets and timber buildings.

Moonlight Sonata

The Coventry Blitz, code named by the Germans as Moonlight Sonata, was the most catastrophic bombing raid. Coventry was the centre of Britain's motor and aviation industry, it also had many munition factories. Germany wanted to obliterate the city.

On the night of 14th November, 1940, 450 bombers dropped 500 tons of high explosives, 30,000 incendiaries, 50 land mines and 20 oil mines. Many thousands of homes were destroyed and three quarters of the city's factories damaged; 554 men, women and children died that night, 865 were injured.

Coventry suffered many bombings during the World War Two, because of armaments, munitions and engine parts factories which played a major part in the British war effort.

The glow from the massive fires as Coventry burned could be seen 80 kilometres away.

From the Ashes

The day after the Blitz, cathedral provost Richard T Howard declared that a new cathedral would be built beside the ruins. The devastated city was visited by King George VI and the prime minister, Sir Winston Churchill. Coventry was one of the finest preserved medieval cities in Europe until the air raids of World War Two. Fortunately some buildings, such as Bond's Hospital and Cheylesmore Manor, escaped with only slight damage. The Council House was relatively lucky only having its windows blown out. Many factories such as Cash's Ribbon Factory and Courtaulds were still smouldering the next day.

However, rebuilding meant that Coventry had Europe's first pedestrian precinct and an awe-inspiring new cathedral designed by Sir Basil Spence. The world's finest craftspeople created magnificent sculptures, beautiful stained and etched glass and a massive tapestry. Queen Elizabeth II came to the new cathedral for its consecration in 1962.

SPOT THIS!

Can you spot this bronze statue of Lady Godiva which was unveiled in 1949? Clue: Try Broadgate where Coventry's castle once stood.

The Jet Engine

Sir Frank Whittle was one of the greatest inventors of the 20th century. He is famous for inventing the jet engine. He was born in Coventry in 1907 and as a child was fascinated by pre-World War One aircraft. After joining the Royal Air Force he was determined to create an aircraft engine that could fly higher and faster than anything ever seen before.

Coventry was also a world leader in manufacturing machine tools – an industry pioneered by Sir Alfred Herbert.

When Frank Whittle and a group of aviation experts watched as a Whittle-Gloster Meteor made its first flight, one man patted Whittle on the back saying: "Frank, it flies!" Frank Whittle replied: "That's what it was designed to do, wasn't it?"

In 1941 a Whittle-Gloster Meteor made its first flight. It reached 8,000 metres and a speed of 600 kph – ground-breaking records in those days.

Reginald is 12 years old. His father is a volunteer fire fighter with the Auxiliary Fire Service. Here is an imaginary diary entry from the Blitz.

Each week, every person was given a ration of 4oz lard or butter, 12oz sugar, 4oz raw bacon or ham and two eggs.

14th November, 1940

7pm We hurried down to the Anderson shelter in our back garden – Mum, my younger brothers and me. We could already hear German aircraft droning overhead and the 'ack-ack' of our anti-aircraft guns. Hundreds of parachute flares falling from the sky. Then came the phosphorous, exploding incendiary bombs, starting fires making us an easy target for the bombers. The bombing went on for 11 hours without a break.

6.15am The all-clear sounded. There wasn't a house in our street that didn't have its roof, doors or windows blown out. Some were nothing but a pile of bricks. We picked our way into town to find Dad. It was drizzling and the streets were just a pile of smouldering rubble. The smell of smoke was heavy in the air. People were wandering about, silent, dazed, exhausted. People cried when they saw the cathedral, it was just a burnt-out shell. Thankfully we found dad, although many fire fighters were killed that night. He was exhausted from fighting fires and pulling the dead and injured from bombed-out buildings.

15th November, 1940

King George VI came to see the destruction, then Sir Winston Churchill. A few days later a mass burial took place in the London Road Cemetery for all the poor people who died that night.

We all 'mucked in' to help with the clear-up. At King Henry VIII school, we had lessons in filling in bomb craters.

Churches, hospitals, schools, shops, railways, houses, factories and even Coventry Cathedral suffered damage in the Blitz.

Today Coventry has two cathedrals. The ruins of St Michael's and the new cathedral stand side by side.

E-type Jaguars outside Browns Lane. Jaguar, British Leyland, Rover, Triumph, Peugeot and Chrysler all had plants in Coventry.

How do we know?

When archaeologists from Birmingham University excavated Bayley Lane, they found an old tin box. Inside were some pre-war pennies and an old wrist-watch. Using local records, they were able to trace relatives of Albert and Elsie Radford who had lived there during the war. You can see their finds at the Herbert Art Gallery and Museum.

Many war survivors have recorded their stories in diaries, letters, newspapers and on radio. So we can learn about the war through the words and experiences of the people who lived through it. Photographs and film reports survive that show us what the city looked like before and after the Blitz.

You can see Frank Whittle's jet engines at the Midlands Air Museum. There is a memorial to the victims of the Coventry Blitz in the London Road Cemetery.

It took years to rebuild the city centre. Now Coventry is a city of Peace and Reconciliation.

Coventry Today and Tomorrow

Today, you can discover Coventry's history for yourself. You can see and touch objects at the Herbert and Transport Museums, visit the Cathedral, walk along the canal, peer at the top shops or join in the Godiva Festival. The important thing to remember is that Coventry's history is about the people who lived through difficult, exciting or dangerous times – people like Marcus, Leofa, Tristana, Benjamin, Alice and Reg!

Someone training at the Coventry Sports and Leisure Centre today could become a famous sports hero of the future.

Will the Frank Whittle Arch still be there in the next millennium?

The Ricoh Arena is the home of Coventry City FC and a venue for great concerts.

The city's Coat of Arms sums up its history. The 'cat-a-mountain' was the emblem of the Black Prince. The motto 'Camera Principis' means 'Prince's Chamber' and refers to his stay in Coventry. The elephant and castle stand for strength. Its back-to-front kneecaps imply that it will not kneel to anyone. The eagle represents the eagle of Leofric and the phoenix symbolizes the city's rise from the ashes of the Blitz.

CAMERA PRINCIPIS

Walk through time at the Transport Museum and see how vehicles have changed.

COVENTRY TRANSPORT MUSEUM

...1987 COVENTRY CITY FC WINS FA CUP...2005 RICOH ARENA OPENS...

You can see objects and pictures from Coventry's past at the Herbert Museum and Art Gallery. What will be displayed from our time for people of the future to see?

King Henry VIII School has been in Warwick Road since 1885. Will it still be there in another 100 years?

SPOT THIS!

Every hour on the hour this mechanical Lady Godiva repeats her famous ride. Can you spot her and Peeping Tom? Clue: You'll find it in Broadgate.

The city's three medieval spires now stand alongside glass and concrete towers on the Coventry skyline.

You can follow a trail and learn about the life of the Coventry poet Philip Larkin.

How will they know?

Will Coventry always look like it does today? How will future generations know what Coventry was like today? The Internet is a great way of recording what Coventry is like now. Photos, blogs and stories from tourists can all spread the word about our wonderful Coventry. Or maybe you'll be famous one day and put Coventry on the map!

The buildings at Coventry University are named after famous Coventry people such as Dame Ellen Terry, James Starley and Frederick Lanchester.

Glossary

Abbey – A religious building where monks or nuns live and work. An Abbot is in charge of the monks, an Abbess is in charge of the nuns.

AD – a short way of writing the Latin words anno Domini, which mean 'in the year of our Lord', i.e. after the birth of Christ.

Anderson shelter – a shelter buried in the garden, where you went for protection when bombs fell in World War Two.

Archaeologist – a person who studies the past by examining buildings and objects left behind by previous people and cultures.

Armaments – weapons and vehicles used for war.

Artefact – another word for an object.

BC – a short way of writing 'before the birth of Christ'.

Benedictine – a monk or nun who joins the Christian religious community that follows the teachings of St Benedict.

Black Death – another name for the plague.

Blacksmith – a person who makes things with iron, such as horseshoes, swords etc.

Blitz – a name for bombing raids by German planes during World War Two.

Cavalry – the part of an army made up of mounted troops, usually on horses but sometimes on elephants or camels.

Church of England – a Christian religion that is headed by the king or queen.

Civil war – a war where people living in the same country fight each other.

Domesday Book – William the Conqueror sent men out to check who owned all the land and wealth in England. The results were written in the Domesday Book, which survives to this day.

Excavation – a site where archaeologists dig up buried objects in order to find out more about the past.

Huguenot – a member of an old French Protestant religion.

Incendiary – anything that causes a fire. In World War Two the Germans dropped incendiary bombs that spread fires and destroyed buildings.

Mason – a person who works with, and makes things from, stone.

Monastery – a place where monks live and worship.

Monk – a male member of a religious community that has rules of poverty, chastity and obedience.

Nunnery – a place where nuns live and worship.

Parliamentarian – anyone who fought on the side of Oliver Cromwell and Parliament in the English Civil War.

Pope – the head of the Roman Catholic Church, which is a Christian religion.

Praetorium – the living quarters of officers of the Roman army.

Ramparts – raised walls or walkways that surround a fort or town.

Royal Charter – written permission from the king or queen to do something.

Royalist – anyone who fought on the side of King Charles I in the English Civil War.

Workhouse – a large building where poor people lived and worked when they had nowhere else to go.

Index

Acknowledgements

The author and publishers would like to thank the following people for their generous help:
Andrew Peel and all at the Lunt Fort for access and all their help;
Coventry Cathedral staff for their kind assistance; Rob Orland for all his kind help;
Damien Kimberley and the Transport Museum for their generosity;
David McGrory for his kind help whilst researching this book.

The publishers would like to thank the following people and organizations
for their permission to reproduce material on the following pages:
p4: Lunt Fort; p5: Lunt Fort; p7: Lunt Fort; p9: Ann Evans, St Mary's Guildhall; p12: St Mary's Guildhall; p13: Mary Evans Picture Library; p14: St Mary's Guildhall; p15: St Mary's Guildhall; p21: Coventry Transport Museum; p22: www.GracesGuide.co.uk/wikipedia, www.victoriansilk.com; p23: Coventry Transport Museum, Alex Askaroff Sewalot Collection; p24: Rob Orland from www.historiccoventry.co.uk; p25: Ian Dunster/Wikipedia; p26: Rob Orland from www.historiccoventry.co.uk; p27: Copyright Jaguar Heritage; p28: David Goddard/Alamy, Lord Mayor's Office Coventry.

Written by Ann Evans
Educational consultant: Neil Thompson
Local history consultant: Roger Bailey
Designed by Stephen Prosser

Illustrated by Kate Davies, Dynamo Ltd, Viriginia Grey, Tim Hutchinson, Peter Kent,
John McGregor, Tim Sutcliffe and Victor McLindon
Additional photographs by Alex Long and Rob Tysall

First published by HOMETOWN WORLD in 2011
Hometown World Ltd
7 Northumberland Buildings
Bath BA1 2JB

www.hometownworld.co.uk

Copyright © Hometown World Ltd 2011

hb ISBN 978-1-84993-116-8
pb ISBN 978-1-84993-150-2

CELT
500 BC

ROMAN
AD 43-410

ANGLO-SAXON
AD 450-1066

VIKING
AD 865-1066

MEDIEVAL TIMES
1066-1485